NEVER AGAIN!

MORE
FASCINATING FACTS
about
IRELAND

Michael Smith

Illustrated by
Nick Scott

WHITE ROW

The White Row Press

NEVER AGAIN!

MORE
FASCINATING FACTS
about
IRELAND

Michael Smith

Illustrated by
Nick Scott

The White Row Press

First published 1999
by the White Row Press
135 Cumberland Road, Dundonald
Belfast BT16 2BB

Typesetting: Island Publications
Printed by the Guernsey Press

A catalogue record for this book is available
from the British Library

ISBN 1 870132 95 5

Contents

Michael Smith *was born in 1966, and moved to Fermanagh at the age of eleven. His spectacularly unsuccessful educational career culminated in a year at the University of Wales, which was spent instead in London and Amsterdam. His working life since has included stints as a plasterer, hotel porter, sometime journalist and tailor. In 1997 he appeared on* Mastermind, *reaching the semifinals. His specialist subject was 16th century Ireland.*

Nick Scott *is a musician and graphic artist. He was cagey about having his age disclosed, and evasive when asked to supply autobiographical details. He lives in Belfast.*

PREFACE

To the Ancient Greeks the island of Ireland was
the domain of the semi-divine Hyperboreans
and the birthplace of the Sun God Apollo. To
the Elizabethans in the 16th century, Ireland and
the Irish were as exotic as the newly discovered
Americas and their native peoples. Although
modern Ireland may have lost much of its
mystery, this book sets out to show that in the
past, and sometimes in the present, fact has
indeed proved stranger than fiction in this
corner of north-west Europe.

NEVER AGAIN! chronicles more than two
hundred and fifty facts – some anecdotal, some
bizarre, some fantastical, but all of them, I hope,
in some way fascinating – relating to Ireland
and its peoples, grouped together in eight
themed chapters covering such diverse subjects
as crime, death, politics and war, all of which
will, hopefully, both amuse and enlighten.

Town and Country takes an off-beat look at the
cityscapes and countryside of Ireland from a

time when there were, quite literally, two Irelands to the present day, as the island makes its stately progress towards the Baltic and, in the process, discovers Flemish in Wexford, Germans in Limerick and a Holy Land in Belfast.

What a Way to Go takes a morbidly wry look at the Irish way of death and how the Grim Reaper cut down, among many others, the killer of Brian Boru and certain of the architects of the Act of Union.

Running to Heaven deals with both the achievements and idiosyncrasies of Ireland's holy men and women and religion in general and, in so doing, places the blame for *The Sound of Music* on an obscure 8th century Irish nun, as well as finding out what links a long submerged island in the River Shannon with the Temples of Abu Simbel in Egypt.

Crime and Punishment brings to book the bad boys and girls of Irish history including the divinely inspired Tipperary teacher who managed to convince an Islamic court that making poitin was an act of worship, and the Dublin women who earned themselves an entry in the august pages of the *Encyclopaedia Britannica*.

The Moxie looks at some of the individuals who have put the 'I' into being Irish, such as Ireland's only Wimbledon champion (to date!), and the Tipperary man who spent two months buried alive in a coffin when he wasn't even dead.

The People have Spoken takes its title from the caustic comment on the vagaries of the democratic process attributed to Mayor Richard J. Daly of Chicago when informed of the election defeat of one of his lieutenants – 'the people have spoken... the bastards!' – and examines the Irish contribution to the second oldest profession.

Universal Soldiers supports the assertion of Hayes-McCoy that the Irish national costume should be a military uniform. It names the County Down man who burned Washington two years after Napoleon burned Moscow, and reveals what Dixie owes to Belfast.

Would you believe it? is a hotchpotch of curious snippets including how news of Eskimos in Galway inspired Columbus to discover the New World, and how an Irishwoman's cow inadvertently caused one of the worst disasters in American history.

The material for *Never Again* has, like that of its predecessor *Never*, come from many sources including the following books which deserve special mention: J. Anderson-Black's *Your Irish Ancestors*; Jonathan Bardon's *A History of Ulster*; Brian Bell and Liam McAuley's *Destination Dublin*; Peter Bowler and Jonathon Green's *What a Way to Go*; Henry Boylan's *A Dictionary of Irish Biography*; Ida Grehan's *Irish Family Names*; D. J. Hickey and J. E. Doherty's *A Dictionary of Irish*

History since 1800; Brendan Lehane's *The Companion Guide to Ireland*; Adrian MacLoughlin's *The City of Belfast, Guide to Historic Dublin* and *Streets of Ireland*; Pat McArt and Donal Campbell's *Irish Almanac and Yearbook of Facts 1997*; Sean McCann's *The Fighting Irish*; Patrick Montague's *Saints and Martyrs of Ireland*; Julia and Brian O'Shea's *Guide to Irish London* and finally Peter Somerville-Large's *Dublin: The First Thousand Years* and *Irish Eccentrics*.

I will leave you with a quote from Shakespeare's Sir John Falstaff:

> 'I am not only witty in myself, but
> the cause that wit is in other men'.

It is in this spirit that this book has been written, and in which it will hopefully be received.

Michael Smith
Drumhack, Lisnaskea

Town and Country

THE first canal in Ireland was built in 1178 by the monks of Claregalway Abbey, County Galway, to create a short cut from their monastery to the mouth of Lough Corrib.

A mysterious explosion near Belleek, County Fermanagh, which left a crater ten feet across but no debris, had army bomb disposal experts completely flummoxed until scientists discovered it had been caused by a meteor fragment just one sixteenth of an inch in diameter.

TULLAMORE, County Offaly, was largely flattened by the explosion of an experimental balloon in 1785.

THE island of Ireland is moving north-eastwards at the rate of an inch per year. In fifty million years time Ireland will be where Denmark is today.

THE 'Catstone' on the Hill of Uisneach in County Westmeath is said to mark the grave of the semi-mythical princess Ériu, after whom Ireland (Erin) is named.

THROUGHOUT the Middle Ages the ownership of Rathlin Island off County Antrim was disputed between Ireland and Scotland. The dispute was finally settled in Ireland's favour in a celebrated court case in 1617, on the grounds that there were no snakes on the island.

THE famous Hill 16 at Croke Park in Dublin was built with rubble taken from Sackville Street (now O'Connell Street) after the 1916 Easter Rising.

IRELAND'S oldest pub is said to be Grace Neill's in Donaghadee, County Down, which was founded in 1611. Among its reputed patrons was Peter the Great, Tsar of Russia, who reputedly popped in for a pint in 1694, during a fact-finding tour of Europe.

COLLEGE Green in Dublin was formerly the site of a Viking cemetery.

IN a remarkable feat of medieval engineering, the River Suck was diverted from its original course to its present one in 1139, for defensive reasons, by the king of Connacht.

Until about 400 million years ago, when two ancient continents collided, Ireland was physically divided into two parts along a line running roughly from what is now Salterstown, County Louth, to the Shannon estuary.

County Mayo takes its name from the village of Mayo near Claremorris. Its abbey was known for many years as 'Mayo of the English' after the English monks who settled there following the triumph of Roman Catholicism over Celtic Christianity at the Synod of Whitby in 664.

THE first ever non-stop transatlantic flight, by the British aviators Alcock & Brown, ended in a crash landing in a bog near Clifden, County Galway.

THE first non-stop solo transatlantic flight by a woman ended when the American aviatrix Amelia Earhart made a perfect landing near Eglington, County Derry, in 1932.

THERE are 40,000 basalt columns in the Giant's Causeway.

DUBHGHALL'S Bridge, the first bridge over the River Liffey in Dublin, was built by the Vikings.

THE world famous Puck Fair, held every August in the County Kerry village of Killorglin, is said to honour the memory of the goat whose bleating warned the villagers of the approach of a hostile Cromwellian army in 1652.

THE remains of the oldest houses in Ireland can be found at Mount Sandel, on the outskirts of Coleraine.

IN the 18th century the taverns of the village of Mungret, now part of Limerick, were renowned for performing rhymers. This is said to have been where the five-lined 'Limerick' was born.

THE Liberties of Dublin are so called because
in the Middle Ages the area lay outside the city
walls and beyond its jurisdiction.

IT was a Belfast tradition for crowds to gather at
the Albert Clock near the Lagan on December
31st and see in the New Year by firing guns into
the air as the ships in the port blared their
hooters.

IRELAND'S first Chamber of Commerce was
founded in Belfast in 1783.

JONATHAN Swift used the name of the long
demolished Lilliput House on the shores of
Lough Ennel, County Westmeath, for the
kingdom of the little people in *Gulliver's Travels*.

THE first case of *phytophthora infestans*, the
blight which caused the Great Famine, occurred
on the estate of the Earl of Erne, at Crom Castle,
County Fermanagh.

THE area east of Queens, in Belfast, has long
been known as 'the Holy Land' because of the
names of three small streets there – Jerusalem,
Damascus, and Palestine Street.

SUCH was the distrust between the two
communities that when Baal's Bridge, or 'the
Bald Bridge' – so called because there were no

Adare, County Limerick, was once known as the Munster Palatinate after the refugees from the Rhenish Palatinate in Germany who settled there in the early 1700s. German surnames such as Ledger, Ruttle, Sparling, and Switzer are still known there.

From 1845 to 1917, Birr, County Offaly, was
home to the world's largest reflecting telescope,
Leviathan, which contained a perfect mirror
72 inches in diameter.

houses on it – was built to link the English and Irish districts of Limerick in 1340, a drawbridge and portcullis gates were installed at each end.

THE first powered flight in Ireland took place from the beach at Newcastle, County Down, on New Year's Eve 1909.

THE oldest part of Ireland is the island of Inishtrahull off County Donegal, whose rocks were formed some 2000 million years ago.

LEOPARDSTOWN, County Dublin, takes its name from an ancient leper colony.

THE Black and Tans, the notorious paramilitary police force deployed by the British government in Ireland in 1920, were named after a pack of foxhounds from the village of Scarteen, County Limerick.

THE world-famous Tara Brooch was found on a beach at Bettystown, County Meath in 1850.

CARNSORE Point in County Wexford was earmarked as the site of the Republic's first nuclear power station until plans were shelved in the face of public opposition.

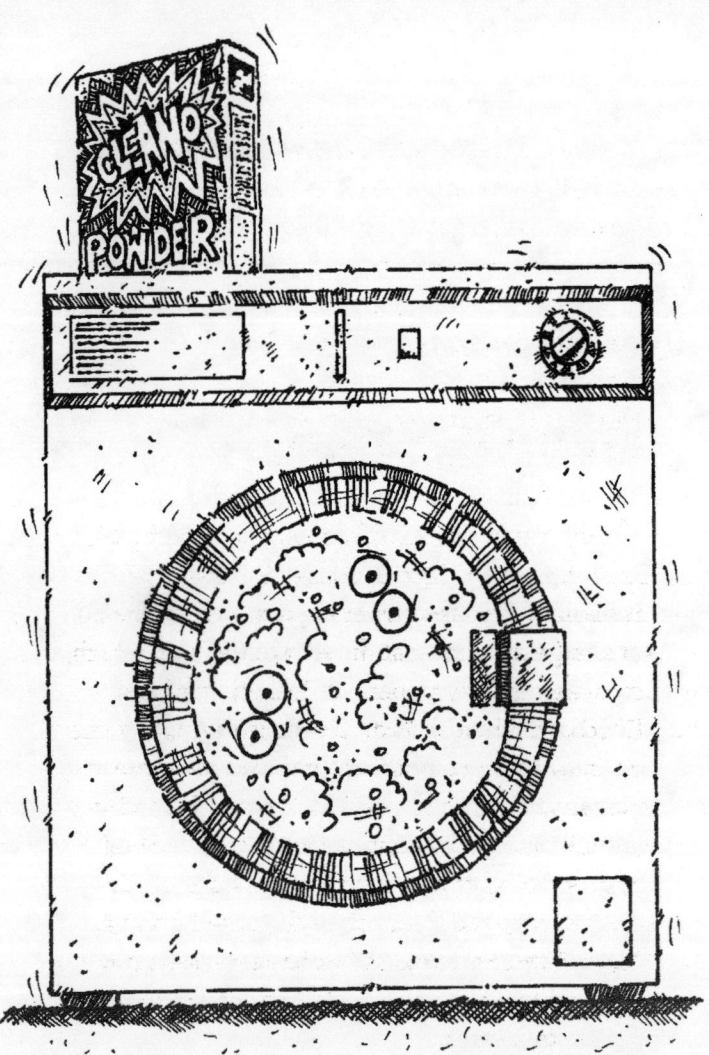

Irish-born tramps Pat Burke and Billy O'Rourke died in St. Louis in 1903, shortly after having had their first baths in twenty years. It was probably not so much the removal of the protective layer of dirt as the fact that the flophouse staff had scrubbed them down with hard bristled brooms which led to the pair's demise.

WHAT A WAY TO GO

AS he lay on his deathbed, surrounded by his family, in the village of Durley in 1654, John Browne was roused from his coma when the lid of a large iron chest at the foot of the bed, which contained family papers, unlocked itself and lifted of its own accord. Sitting upright, Browne addressed the open chest thus, 'You say true, you say true, you say right. I'll be with you by and by'. He then collapsed back onto the bed and as the lid of the chest closed and the locks on it re-engaged themselves, breathed his last. No satisfactory explanation has ever been put forward for this well-attested manifestation of the supernatural.

THE first recorded shipwreck in Irish waters was in 440, when an Irish war fleet was lost off Rathlin Island.

TIGERMAS, the founder of a cruel Irish cult which demanded the sacrifice of first-born adults and children to satisfy the Worm God, was put to death by his own frenzied followers when they found out that he was an eldest son.

THE Viking warlord Turgesius, who terrorised Ireland between 831-45, levied arbitrary taxes on those he defeated including a so-called 'nose tax'. Defaulters were punished by having their noses cut off.

IRELAND'S first possible 'UFO' sighting occurred in 749 when, 'Ships with their crews were seen in the air over Clonmacnoise'.

THE last stop Michael Collins made on his fateful tour of inspection in 1922 was at the National Army outpost at Bandon, which was commanded by Major General Sean Hales. From there he drove to Béal na mBláth where he was killed in an ambush laid by republicans under the command of Tom Hales, Sean's brother.

AS he lay on his deathbed in a cheap boarding house in Paris, Oscar Wilde uttered the famous last words, 'Either this wallpaper goes or I do.' The wallpaper stayed.

MISFORTUNE befell all the principal architects of the Act of Union. After his death in 1802 the coffin of the Earl of Clare was followed

The youngest British Army casualty of the First World War was Private John Condon of the Royal Irish Regiment, who was just fourteen when he died at Ypres in 1915.

One of the longest chess matches on record took place between Belfast grandmaster, Alexander McDonnell, and the French champion, de Labourdonnai. Beginning in 1834, it dragged on for more than a year with first one man and then the other getting the upper hand. The Frenchman secured victory when his opponent dropped dead on the eve of the 89th game.

to the grave by a cursing mob. Lord Kilwarden
was piked to death during the rebellion of 1803.
Lord Castlereagh cut his throat with a paper
knife in 1822 during a bout of deep depression.

THE Viking berserker who killed Brian Boru at
the Battle of Clontarf was reputedly put to death
by having his stomach slit open, and one end of
his entrails tied to a tree, which he was forced
around until he was completely disembowelled.

THE last person to be burned at the stake in
Britain was an Irishwoman by the name of
Murphy who was executed in 1789 for the crime
of 'petty treason' i.e. killing her husband. She
was strangled before the fire was lit.

AN estimated 14,000 people died when the
Black Death struck Ireland in 1348.

THE most famous Irish 'witch' was Dame Alice
Kyteler who lived in Kilkenny in the 14th
century. A wealthy widow, she was accused by
the avaricious Bishop of Ossary of poisoning her
four husbands, presiding over black masses, and
turning her negro manservant into a cat. Dame
Alice escaped to England with the help of some
well-connected friends. Her maid Petronella
was not so lucky, she was burned at the stake in
place of her mistress. Dame Alice's house is a
tourist attraction in modern Kilkenny.

MORE than 150 people were killed when a barge carrying gunpowder accidentally exploded at Wood Quay in Dublin in 1596.

DURING the siege of Carrickfergus Castle by Edward the Bruce in 1316, eight Scots prisoners were reportedly killed and eaten by the starving garrison.

WHEN a Russian shell tore open his chest during the Charge of the Light Brigade, the Irish cavalry officer Lewis Nolan was returned to his own lines by his horse, sitting bolt upright in the saddle with his sword arm raised – a victim of cadaveric spasm, or instant *rigor mortis*.

IN 1584 a gladiatorial contest was held in the courtyard of Dublin Castle in order to settle a long running dispute between two Irish chieftains. The victor cut off his rival's head and presented it to the watching Lord Justice of Ireland as a grisly trophy.

IRELAND'S worst shipwreck was that of the Spanish Armada galleon *Girona*, which went down off north Antrim during a storm in 1588. All but nine of the 1,300 or so men aboard were drowned in the boiling sea.

MAJOR Denis Mahon has gone down in history as one of the villains of the Great

Armagh-born Sir Daniel O'Neill was appointed Royal Alehouse Regulator by his friend Charles II in 1660, a post which entitled him to free drink in any tavern in England. So diligent was he in his duties that he died of cirrhosis of the liver in 1664.

Alexander Pierce of County Monaghan, who had
been transported to Van Diemen's Land in 1819,
escaped from prison with five other convicts in
1822. Once in the bush, however, the convicts
became hopelessly lost. As the days went by and
hunger got the better of him, Pierce began picking
off his companions one by one, killing and eating
them all before giving himself up. Four months
later, Pierce went on the run again, this time with
a prisoner named Cox, whom he also devoured.
Appalled by the Irishman's fondness for the taste of
human flesh, and fearful for themselves during the
long trek back, his captors hanged the cannibalistic
Pierce on the spot.

Famine, and was shot dead for his 'crimes' in
1847. In fact, Mahon went deep into debt to pay
the fares of those tenants on his Strokestown
estate who wanted to emigrate to America. He
even provided them with free food for the
crossing. Mahon's downfall, however, came
with an outbreak of typhus on the emigrant
ship, during which half his tenants perished.
When the news reached Ireland some weeks
later, the relatives of the dead swore vengeance
and the luckless major's fate was sealed.

HAVING failed to commit suicide by slitting
his throat after being sentenced to death in 1798,
Wolfe Tone lingered in agony with a half
severed windpipe for more than a week until he
overheard a visiting surgeon remark that it
would be fatal for the prisoner to attempt to
speak. Tone whispered, 'I can yet find word to
thank you, sir, it is the most welcome news you
could give me.' He then died.

WHEN one Brian Maguire was found dead in
a barn in Finglas, County Dublin, in 1835, the
mummified body of his long dead and much
loved baby son was found alongside him.

IN November 1810, twenty-two people were
killed in an explosion in Brandy Lane, Cork,
when a man who had been stealing gunpowder
and storing it in the cellar of his house went to

inspect his haul – with a lighted candle.

AFTER his death, the body of Marcus Keane , a
bailiff who had evicted large numbers from the
Kilrush area of County Clare during the Famine,
was dug up and thrown onto a dung heap.

FORTY-FOUR year-old Irishwoman Bridget
Driscoll achieved the dubious distinction of
becoming the first traffic accident fatality of the
modern age when she was run over and killed
by a car careering along at four miles per hour in
Croydon, south London, in 1896.

IRELAND'S worst train crash occurred near
Markethill in 1889 when an engine ran out of
steam on a steep hill and rolled back down into
an oncoming train killing more than eighty
people, many of them children on a Sunday
School excursion.

WHEN the newly appointed Lord Deputy of
Ireland, the Earl of Essex, arrived in Dublin in
1599, the leading citizens of the city were rowed
out to greet him. Their boat capsized in the
middle of the Liffey and twenty were drowned.

SUCH was his fear of being buried alive that
the celebrated churchman and eccentric Philip
Skelton ordered that his throat be cut after his
death to make sure he was really dead. It was.

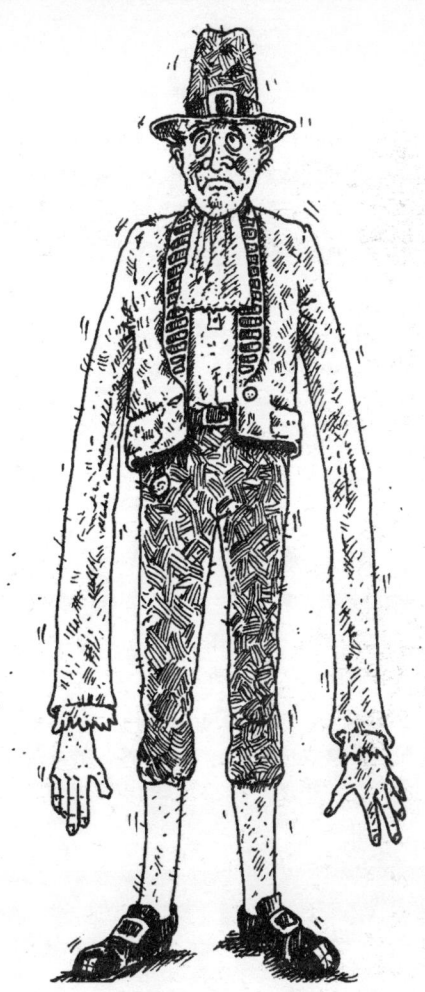

*Peter Harkan, a 19th century 'Resurrection Man',
whose job was to supply the surgeons of the Meath
Hospital in Dublin with fresh cadavers for study,
met his end while grave robbing. As he tried to
escape over a cemetery wall after being caught
digging up a freshly buried body, Harkan's legs
were grabbed by a night watchman while his arms
were grabbed by his partners in crime. Harken
suffered fatal internal injuries during the ensuing
tug of war.*

OF the approximately 500,000 Irishmen who fought in the two World Wars, some 60,000 were killed in action.

THE celebrated 18th century Irish beauty Lady Maria Coventry died in 1760, having been slowly poisoned by lead in the make up she wore to give her skin the white porcelain tone for which she was so famous.

THE garrison of Limerick surrendered in 1651 after being betrayed by one of their own officers, Colonel Fennell. To punish their defiance, the victors randomly picked out twenty-four of the unfortunate defenders and hanged them – amongst them was the treacherous Fennell.

Running to Heaven

IRELAND'S largest church is in Knock, County Mayo. It has a capacity of 12,000.

IN the classic John Wayne film *The Quiet Man*, there is a scene in which the local priest saves his Church of Ireland counterpart from being moved by his bishop because of poor attendances at his services by ordering his parishioners to pack the church on the day the bishop came to visit, and to pass themselves off as devout protestants. This piece of cinematic fiction is based on an actual incident which occurred in Belleek, County Fermanagh, in the mid 19th century, when the village priest, Fr. Ryan helped his friend, the Rev. Tuthill, out of exactly the same predicament using the same subterfuge.

CHARLEMAGNE'S civil service was trained by Irish monks.

More than 11,000 priests have graduated from St. Patrick's College in Maynooth since its foundation in 1795.

THE eminent medieval theologian Duns Scottus from County Down was so renowned for his advocacy of traditional Catholic doctrine that the early protestant reformers dubbed anyone who opposed them as a 'Duns', hence the term 'dunce' for a slow learner.

THE bones of St. Valentine, who gave his name to Valentine's day, are kept in the Whitefriar Church, Dublin.

IRISH nuns made up twenty of the thirty-eight nurses who worked in Florence Nightingale's hospital during the Crimean War.

WHILE baptising Aengus, King of Cashel, in 445, St. Patrick unwittingly stuck the spike of his crozier through his new convert's foot. When later asked why he had not cried out, Aengus replied that he thought it was part of the ceremony.

SOME forty years before the Egyptians moved the temples of Abu Simbel clear of the waters of the Aswan Dam, a similar feat of engineering was carried out on an early medieval church on an island in the Shannon, to make way for the Shannon hydro-electric scheme in 1929.

AMONGST the 1,400 named Irish saints are 18 Fintans, 11 Bridgets, and 120 Colmans.

HAVING vowed never again to set foot on Ireland, St. Columcille returned frequently, but got round his vow by having two sods cut from the soil of Iona made into sandals.

ARMAGH Cathedral was burned in 1566 – by its own priests.

BOTH the legend of King Arthur and that of the Holy Grail were largely the creation of the Irish monks who founded Glastonbury in Somerset in the 6th century.

THE most successful temperance crusade in history was that led by the Irish priest Fr. Mathew. It began in Cork in 1838, and by 1844 some five million people had taken the pledge.

THE Synod of Kells divided Ireland up into thirty-six dioceses, each of which had access to either the Shannon or the sea.

IRELAND'S last hermit was Patrick Beglin, who lived amongst the ruins of Fore Abbey in County Westmeath until his death in 1616.

THE priest who accompanied Louis XVI of France to the guillotine on the day of his execution was Henry Edgeworth from Longford.

Many historians believe that the Irish monk St. Brendan was the first European to reach North America, which he did in about 570, beating Christopher Columbus by over nine centuries.

The Nonnberg convent near Salzberg in Austria, now best known for its association with **The Sound of Music,** was founded by the 8th century Irish nun Erintrude.

TWO hundred monks were killed in a pitched battle between the rival monasteries of Clonmacnoise and Durrow in 760.

UNTIL its suppression by Pope Alexander VI, St. Patrick's Purgatory on Lough Derg was one of the great devotional centres of Christendom. Pilgrims came from across Europe to be locked inside a pitch black cave from which it was said that they could communicate with the souls of the dead.

IN early medieval Ireland, important testimonies were sworn on the crozier of St. Dymphna, which was kept in a monastery in County Monaghan. It was believed that anyone who swore a false oath on the relic would have their mouth twisted out of shape, thus marking them out as a liar for the rest of their lives.

A 7th century Irish law tract forbade working on a Sunday on pain of a fine of one year's wages.

THE private one-to-one confession of the Catholic Church has its origin in Irish penitential practice, which was introduced into Europe by Irish missionaries in the 8th century. Prior to that time confession was made in public in front of a crowd.

*According to tradition, pre-Christian Ireland had
five great roads. One ran from what is now
Dublin to Galway. The other four linked the hill of
Tara with Kerry, Armagh, the south coast near
Waterford, and Rathcroghan, in County
Roscommon, the ancient capital of Connacht.*

CRIME AND PUNISHMENT

TIPPERARYMAN M.J. O'Reilly was arrested
for making poitin in Lybia in 1977. He escaped
prison and a public flogging when he somehow
convinced the court that he had been engaged in
a religious ritual in honour of St. Patrick.

THE 12th century warlord Dermot
MacMurrough settled a long running dispute
over who should be abbess of the shrine of St.
Bridget at Kildare by raping the incumbent,
ensuring that she would be compelled to leave
office as she was no longer a virgin.

IN the 16th century the Archbishop of Cashel
employed a notorious pirate, Fineen O'Driscoll,
to attack ships trying to enter Waterford
harbour, and to force them up the River Suir to
Carrick so that he could collect their customs
duty for himself.

THE favourite hobby of the Irish-American

gangster Dion O'Bannion was flower arranging.
Wreaths to the value of $100,000 were bought
from his florists in Chicago after he was gunned
down on Al Capone's orders in 1924.

CAPTURED by his bitter enemy Shane O'Neill
in 1561, Calvagh O'Donnell, lord of Tyrconnell,
had a collar placed round his neck which was
chained to fetters on his ankles in such a way
that he could neither sit, stand upright or lie
down flat. When he was released two years
later he was both mentally and physically a
broken man.

BEFORE the opening of the Four Courts in
1802, the Dublin courts of justice were situated
within the precincts of St. Patrick's Cathedral.

IN a notably grave breach of hospitality, the
Earl of Essex had 300 members of the ruling
Clannaboy O'Neill clan put to death after luring
them to a feast in Belfast Castle in 1573.

LANDMARKS amongst the IRA's
contributions to urban redevelopment include
the destruction of Nelson's Pillar in O'Connell
Street in 1966, a statue of William III blown off
its pedestal outside Trinity College in 1929, and
an equestrian statue of George II in Phoenix
Park meeting the same fate in 1937.

The only punishment for crime in ancient Ireland was a fine known as an éraic. It was paid by the wrongdoer to his victim and equated to that person's 'honour price'. The honour price of a freeman was six heifers, three cows or one female slave.

H.M.P. MAZE

XMAS
PANTO
SNOW WHITE
AND THE
SEVEN
DWARVES

*The level of prisoner control in the Maze prison –
supposedly the most secure in Europe – was such
that the IRA men digging an escape tunnel in
1977 didn't bother thinking of ingenious ways of
disposing of the soil. They simply piled it up in
two empty cells, confident that no guard would
enter without the permission of their H block
commander.*

BALTIMORE in County Cork was raided by Algerian pirates in 1631. Two hundred of the townspeople were carried into captivity. No-one ever returned.

THE Irish-born St. Fiacre is the patron saint of haemorrhoid sufferers. He died at Meaux in France, and went on to become the patron saint of the French royal family. Louis XIV, 'the Sun King', was said to be particularly devoted to the Irishmen's memory.

THE Canadian 'Mounties' were founded by Roscommon man George French in 1873.

IN 1641 Owen O'Connolly received £500 for informing the authorities of a plot by Conor Maguire and Hugh MacMahon to seize Dublin Castle. In 1644 Maguire and MacMahon escaped from the Tower of London, where they were awaiting trial for treason. They were recaptured after being spotted wandering along Drury Lane by Owen O'Connolly who by sheer chance happened to be in London. He picked up a further £200 for his trouble.

ST. Stephen's Green in Dublin was formerly the site of the city's public executions.

IRISHMAN James Quinn acted on the London stage in the early 1700s. Notoriously highly strung, he killed two fellow thespians in duels, one after a row over the proper pronunciation of the name of the character Cato in Shakespeare's *Julius Caesar*.

THE South Seas Company, which collapsed in 1720 in the greatest financial scandal in British history, was founded by the Monaghan-born financier Arthur Moore in 1710. He had the 'foresight' to sell just before the crash.

ONE of the most famous illegal pirate radio stations of them all, Radio Caroline, was the brainchild of the Dublin entrepreneur Ronan O'Rahilly. Whilst fitting out his ship in County Louth, he ensured total secrecy by telling the staunchly republican locals that his 'spy ship' would be used to track the movements of the Royal Navy for the IRA.

THE notorious pirate Anne Bonney, who terrorised the Spanish Main in the 1720s, was born in County Cork in 1697. When captured she was spared execution because she was pregnant.

MAJOR Ronald Bunting was one of the Rev. Ian Paisley's most ardent supporters during the 1960s. His son Ronald, however, joined the INLA, and was one of its leaders at the time of his assassination in 1980.

'Monto' (short for Montgomery Street), the district behind what is now Dublin's Connolly Station, was such a notorious red-light district in the latter half of the 19th century that it managed to earn a place as such in the Encyclopedia Britannica. At its height some 1,600 prostitutes worked there, catering for the carnal needs of, amongst others, the city's ten thousand strong garrison.

As late as 1930 over one-third of New York's policemen were Irish.

IN an act of almost unbelievable mental cruelty, the Earl of Belvedere had his young wife, whom he suspected of being unfaithful, imprisoned in his ancestral home on the shores of Lough Ennel in County Westmeath. For thirty-one years she was forbidden all human contact except with servants who were not allowed to speak to her. When her ordeal finally ended in 1774 with the death of her husband, she was released half mad, unable to speak properly and still wearing the same faded clothes that had been the height of fashion three decades before.

THE Book of Kells was stolen in 1006. When it was recovered three months later sixty of its pages and its original gold embossed cover were missing. They were never found.

THE famous Dublin actress Peg Woffington (1714-60) settled a long running feud with her bitter rival Mrs Bellamy by stabbing her with a sword prop and then pushing her off the stage in the middle of a performance.

THOUSANDS of Irish beggars were shipped to the West Indies in the 1650s.

IRELAND'S only ever pogrom took place in Limerick in 1904, when, after listening to a fiery sermon on the evils of usury, a mob went on the rampage attacking the homes and businesses of the city's thirty or so leading Jewish families, forcing them to flee for their lives.

THE illegality of poitín-making dates from 1760 when an Act of Parliament made the unlicensed private distillation of whiskey an offence.

DURING the crackdown which preceded the 1798 rebellion a militia sergeant known as 'Tom the Devil' devised the torture known as 'cropping'. This involved covering the suspect's head in molten pitch, and pulling the pitch cap off after it had hardened.

IN 1830 magistrates in County Roscommon appointed Ireland's only ever hang-woman, who was known only by the pseudonym 'Lady Betty'.

IRELAND'S very own 'crown jewels', which consist of a jewelled star, a diamond brooch and five gold collars, all regalia of the now defunct Order of St. Patrick, were stolen from Dublin Castle in 1907. They have never been recovered.

THE IRA gang who raided the armoury of Felstead public school in Essex in 1953 loaded their van so heavily with weapons that when they tried to make their getaway they found that it would hardly move. The van was overtaken by the local bobby on his bicycle, and its occupants arrested.

The Moxie

The Rev. Charles Bunworth of Buttevant, County Cork, was a generous patron and friend to many poor itinerant harpers. On his death fifteen harps were discovered in the loft of his granary, bequeathed to him by the last members of a dying tradition. The harps were broken up to feed his successor's cooking fires.

The socialist anthem *The Red Flag* was written by Meathman, Jim Connell.

Over three million Irish trees are estimated to have been flattened during the 'Night of the Big Wind' in 1839.

Robert Cook (d. 1726), squire of Cappoquin in County Waterford, was an eccentric whose obsessive fondness for the colour white led him to wear only white clothes, ride only white horses, and have only white cattle on his farm.

Marie Louise Murphy, the daughter of an Irish Brigade veteran, became the mistress of Louis XV of France after he saw a naked portrait of her by Boucher. She survived three stormy marriages and imprisonment during the French Revolution to die in her sleep in 1814.

RORY O'Connor, who reigned from 1169-84 was the last High King of Ireland.

WHEN Johnny comes marching home, the unofficial anthem of the American Civil War, was written by a Dubliner.

IN 1626, Mary Stuart O'Donnell, daughter of the Earl of Tyrconnell, fled Ireland dressed as a man to escape an arranged marriage. Despite marrying twice, she continued to dress and behave like a man in public for the rest of her life.

THE first Irishman to climb Mount Everest was Belfast's Dawson Stelfox.

THE captain of the ship which carried King James to France after the Battle of the Boyne was an Irishman by the name of Philip Walsh. His son brought 'the Young Pretender', Bonnie Prince Charlie to Scotland in 1745.

THE Irish tenor John McCormick was the first singer to earn more than a million dollars.

THE British Museum was founded in 1753 with the 55,000 books, manuscripts and curios of the County Down-born physician Sir Hans Sloane. His equally impressive botanical collection established Kew Gardens six years later. Sloane

Square in London is named after him.

JOHN Lennon was named after his Dublin-born grandfather who toured the United States as a travelling singer before settling in Liverpool.

THE Waterford-born actress Dorothy Jordan had ten illegitimate children by the Duke of Clarence, who became William IV in 1830. She was rewarded with a pension of £1,000 per annum. When the stingy Clarence tried to reduce this amount, she famously sent him the bottom half of a play-bill which read, 'No money returned after the rising of the curtain'.

THE Dublin-born writer Bram Stoker, who created Dracula in 1897, used his own insomnia as the basis of the vampire's fear of daylight.

WHEN his second wife's pet dog died, the 18th century Antrim landlord Clotworthy Skeffington threw a lavish funeral service for it, attended by fifty other dogs, decked out in mourning.

ANGINA was first diagnosed by the Newry physician Samuel Black.

ON the eve of the Great Famine Ireland had the lowest average marriage age in Europe, sixteen for girls, seventeen for boys.

*Dubliner Dan Donnelly became the first
recognised world boxing champion when he beat
Englishman George Cooper in an epic bare knuckle
bout fought at the Curragh, County Kildare, in
1815.*

The 1967 Censorship Act, which restricted the powers of the Republic's Censorship Board, released 5,000 previously forbidden tomes to the Irish book buying public.

A notorious money lender by the name of Bruce, who operated in Limerick in the 1770s, had an iron leg which he would tap when debtors begged for mercy, telling them, 'That's the softest part of me'.

CATHERINE Kelly (1756-85) was known as 'the Irish Fairy'. She was only 34 inches tall and never weighed more than twenty-two pounds.

QUATERNIONS, the numerical formulae upon which quantum mechanics are based, and without which Einstein could not have calculated the Theory of Relativity, were the brainchild of Irish mathematician Sir William Rowan Hamilton.

THE obscure German writer who created the compulsively boastful Baron Munchausen is buried in Killarney, where he died while prospecting for copper in 1794.

ALTHOUGH born with only the rudiments of arms and legs, the extraordinary Carlowman Arthur Kavanagh became one of the first Europeans to explore central Asia, a feat which he accomplished in the company of a Russian dwarf. He rounded off his career by becoming MP for Carlow.

GALWAY-born Robert Burke walked the 1,500

miles north-south across Australia to win a bet in 1860. He died of starvation on the return journey.

JULIA Kavanagh (1824-77) was the first Irishwoman to make her living from writing.

THE blind harpist Denis Hempson, who died in 1807 at the reputed age of 112, was known as the man with two heads, there being a large excrescence on the back of his head. He is always pictured wearing a hat.

JOHN Doherty of Donegal became the world's first trade union leader in 1829.

DUNGAL of Bangor, an astronomer at the court of Charlemagne, was the first person to understand the previously feared phenomenon of the solar eclipse.

THE modern London Fire Brigade is the creation of the Corkman Sir Eyre Massey-Shaw, who in 1861 took over a service largely unchanged since the Fire of London, and turned it into the most technologically advanced force in the world.

TIPPERARY barman Mike Meaney spent sixty-one days buried alive in a coffin eleven feet under a London pub for a bet in 1968.

Wicklowman Joshua Pim was the first and last Irishman to win Wimbledon, taking the Men's Singles title in 1893 and 1894.

THE PEOPLE HAVE SPOKEN

IN 1921 both Michael Collins and Eamon de Valera were elected to the Northern Ireland parliament for seats in counties Armagh and Down respectively. To the relief, perhaps, of Unionists, neither man took his seat.

DUBLIN was given the right to appoint its own mayor and corporation by Henry III in 1229 in return for writing off a loan.

UNLIKE their English, Scottish, Welsh and Northern Irish counterparts, peers from the Irish Republic can sit in the House of Commons.

THE leaders of the 'Tweed Ring' which controlled New York City politics between 1868-71, during which time a staggering $200,000,000 went missing from public coffers, were Irishmen Richard Connolly and Richard Sweeney, both of whom escaped arrest when the ring was smashed. Connolly fled to Europe with

One of the most zealous children of the French Revolution was the Irish-born swordsman John O'Sullivan. During the Reign of Terror he executed his royalist brother and ordered the so-called enemies of the state to be chained to barges which he had towed out and sunk in the River Loire. The Committee of Public Safety cleared him of any wrongdoing on the grounds that he was 'merely a good revolutionary with a perverted moral sense'.

The fourteen merchant families, the so-called
'Tribes' who controlled the political and
commercial life of medieval Galway, and gave the
city its nickname, were Athy, Blake, Bodkin,
Browne, D'Arcy, Deane, Font, French Joyce,
Kirwin, Lynch, Martin, Morris and Skerrit.

$6,000,000 in a suitcase, while Sweeney cut a deal which let him to keep $400,000 of what he had embezzled, enough to allowed him spend the rest of his days in luxury in Paris.

THE first Irish parliament was held at Castledermot, County Kildare in 1264.

IN 1920 an estimated 100,000 Londoners filed past the coffin of IRA hunger striker and Lord Mayor of Cork, Terence MacSwiney as it lay in Southwark Cathedral. He had died after going without food for 74 days.

IN 1447 the wearing of moustaches was made illegal in Ireland.

THE briefest parliamentary career ever was that of Young Irelander John Mitchell, who was elected for North Tipperary in 1874 only to have his victory annulled because he was a convicted felon. Re-elected with an increased majority, Mitchel dropped dead while celebrating his victory.

WILLIAM, Duke of Windsor, who was appointed Justiciar of Ireland in 1369, used ingenious methods to raise taxes from Irish parliaments. He called one in the middle of nowhere and starved its members into submission, while at another he had everyone locked up until they agreed with him.

ALL bar one of the leaders of the republican United Irishmen were protestants.

ATTORNEY General Patrick Connolly, the Republic's chief law officer, resigned in 1982 after a double murder suspect was found in his apartment.

AFTER his death in 1469, the beloved Mayor Rice of Waterford ordered that his coffin be opened after a year, and a likeness be made of his decaying corpse to show the citizenry that he was as human as they. This hideous likeness can still be seen in Christchurch Cathedral.

IN 1925 the new Prime Minister of Northern Ireland, Sir James Craig, was presented with a gold mounted portion of a foot-rule by Belfast shipyard workers representing the inch that went unyielded during the partition negotiations.

THERE were so many Irish exiles living in Galicia in the 17th century that Philip III of Spain appointed one of his ministers 'Protector of the Irish' to deal exclusively with their affairs.

SO powerful was the Cork-born politician, Richard 'Boss' Croker, grand sachem of the New

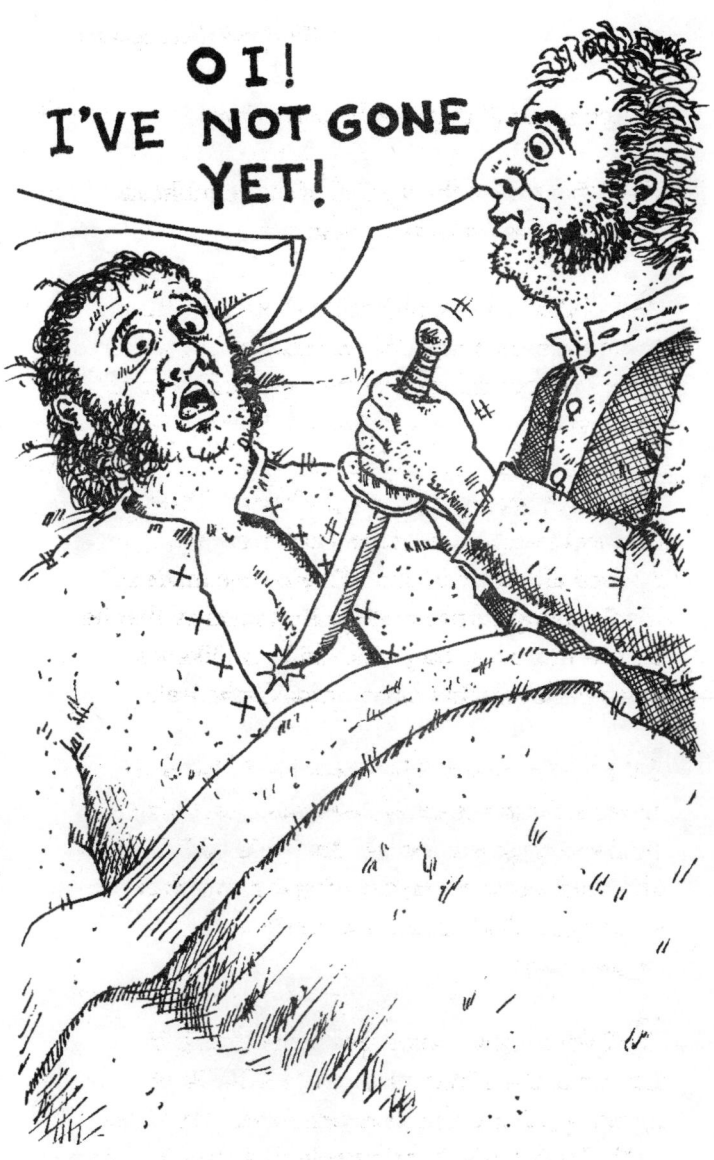

Upon his death in 1847, Daniel O'Connell's body went to Ireland for burial while his heart was sent to Rome for a separate interment.

A staggering £1,260,000 was paid out by the British government to smooth the passage of the Act of Union in 1800.

York political machine, that from 1894 until his enforced retirement in 1902, he ruled the city by telegram from his country estate in England.

THE word 'Tory' derives from the Irish word for bandit. It has been used to denote a member of the Conservative Party since the 1670s.

THE American Declaration of Independence was drafted by Charles Thompson of Derry, printed by John Dunlap of Strabane, and first signed by John Hancock , whose ancestors came from County Down.

Universal Soldiers

THE parents of the legendary American frontiersman, Davy Crockett, were from Castlederg, County Tyrone.

ANCIENT Irish warriors suffered a form of post-traumatic stress known as 'geilt'. The earliest sufferer was the warlord Buile Suibhne who was driven insane by the carnage he had witnessed at the Battle of Moira in 637.

THE liberation of occupied Europe was begun by soldiers of the Inniskilling Fusiliers who landed on Sicily in July 1943.

FORBIDDEN by law to engage in physical combat, poets in ancient Ireland did their bit by composing 'defamations' and 'maledictions' which they recited at the enemy before battle.

EIGHT Irish pilots were among 'The Few' who

No fewer than four south American navies, those of Argentina, Ecuador, Uruguay and Chile, were founded by Irishmen.

*More than 120,000 American servicemen and
women were stationed in Northern Ireland
between 1942-45.*

fought in the Battle of Britain in 1940. All survived.

THE opponents of the Roman invaders of Britain included the Ulster chieftain Calgach, an outstanding warrior admired by Tacitus.

GETTYSBURG, Pennsylvania, which in 1863 was the site of the bloodiest battle of the American Civil War, was named after John Getty, who settled there after emigrating from Derry in 1791.

GEORGE Woulfe, the great-grandfather of the military hero General James Wolfe, who won Canada for Britain at the Battle of Quebec, was executed for the part he played in defending Limerick against English troops in 1651.

THE bloodiest battle fought on Irish soil was Aughrim, in 1691, in which over 6,000 died.

THE last invasion of Britain took place in 1797, when a French expeditionary force under Irish-born General William Tate came ashore at Fishguard in Wales. They surrendered within hours, believing themselves to be surrounded by British soldiers in the surrounding hills. The 'soldiers' were in fact local women in their traditional costume of black stovepipe hat and scarlet shawl.

TWENTY-six ships of the Spanish Armada were wrecked off Ireland in 1588.

THE IRA Bishopsgate bomb, which devastated the City of London in 1993, caused damage conservatively estimated at £800,000,000 – more than all the bombs which have exploded in Northern Ireland combined.

THE Beaufort Scale, which is used to measure wind strength, was devised by Captain Francis Beaufort from Navan, County Meath.

'LAWRENCE of Arabia' was not English. He was born in Wales, the son of a dissolute Irishman who fled the country when news of his affair with his children's governess became public knowledge.

RULES of war aimed at protecting the lives of non-combatants were laid down by the Irish holyman St. Adamnan in 697.

THE world's first war correspondent was the Dublin-born journalist Sir William Howard Russell, who wrote for *The Times*. He broke the news of the ill-fated charge of the Light Brigade, and turned Florence Nightingale into a national heroine.

THE so-called 'Butter Captains' were officers

Twenty-five year-old Oliver Walsh of Kilkenny was the youngest of Nelson's captains at Trafalgar.

sent to Hugh O'Neill by Elizabeth I to train six companies of his men to police Ulster for the crown. By constantly changing the composition of the companies, the wily rebel got an army several thousand strong trained in the use of the musket and the pike.

THE only Irish recipient of the Dicken Medal, the animal VC, was Paddy the carrier pigeon, the first bird to reach London with the news of the D Day landings in 1944.

CROMWELL'S only defeat in Ireland was at Clonmel, where his forces were repulsed by two hundred Ulstermen under Hugh Duff O'Neill. That night O'Neill's men quietly slipped away, allowing the mayor to surrender the unbreached town the following morning. This meant that under the rules of 17th century warfare to which he scrupulously adhered, Cromwell had no choice but to give the inhabitants quarter.

THE Byerley Turk, the Arab stallion from which all modern racehorses are ultimately descended, fought at the Battle of the Boyne in 1690.

AFTER surrendering Singapore to the Japanese in 1942, the defeated British commander Lt. General Percival received a gloating telegram from Tom Barry, the IRA commandant whom

In East Tyrone in 1988, members of an army foot patrol were saved from certain death when a cow chewed through a command wire running from a hilltop firing point to an IRA landmine buried in a roadside culvert.

Percival had so ruthlessly pursued in west Cork
during the War of Independence twenty years
before.

THERE has been an army camp at the Curragh
since 1646.

MOST of the ships which ran the blockade of
Confederate ports, bringing supplies to the
beleaguered South during the American Civil
War, were built at Harland & Wolff in Belfast,
where revolutionary advances in hull design,
the so-called 'Belfast bottom', gave them the
advantage over pursuing federal warships.

DUBLIN Castle was stormed by republicans
during the 1916 Easter Rising. The attackers
bound and gagged six soldiers they surprised in
the guardroom, then beat a hasty retreat,
unaware that they had overwhelmed three-
quarters of the entire garrison.

THERE was a protestant company of the IRA in
Belfast in the 1930s, led by John Graham from
the Antrim Road.

TWO years after Napoleon captured and
burned Moscow in 1812, a British army under
the County Down soldier Robert Ross captured
and burned Washington.

Archbishop Thomas Croke, after whom Croke Park in Dublin is named, was a liberal-minded prelate who, as a young priest studying in France, fought on the barricades during the 1848 revolution.

*Pope Alexander VIII celebrated William's victory
at the Battle of the Boyne with a Te Deum, and the
ringing of church bells throughout Rome.*

BOTH wings of Brian Boru's army at the Battle of Clontarf in 1014 – which destroyed Viking power in Ireland – were, ironically, commanded by Vikings.

THE most cosmopolitan conflict in Irish history was the Williamite War (1689-91), which involved soldiers from Denmark, England, France, Germany, Holland, Poland, Sweden and Switzerland. The vast majority of casualties were, however, Irish.

AFTER his death in battle in 1599, the English general Sir Conyers Clifford was decapitated by his enemies, who then buried his head with elaborate ceremony on an island in Lough Key, County Roscommon.

NORMAN military operations in Ireland did not begin in 1169. A small raiding party led by Richard Fitz Godebert actually landed in the country two years earlier.

WOULD YOU BELIEVE IT?

THE Belfast-born scientist Lord Kelvin designed the first modern battleship, the *HMS Dreadnought* in 1906.

IRISH Brehon law permitted a man to have three 'wives' – a principal wife, a concubine and a mistress.

BEFORE the Education Act of 1832 established the National School System, there were some nine thousand 'hedge schools' in Ireland.

WHILE writing his classic *Commentary* on the Gallic Wars, Caesar mistook the Latin word for 'wintry' (hibernus) for the Roman name for Ireland (Iuverna). No-one dared to correct the great man's error, and the name Hibernia stuck.

IN the 1920s the Rath of Synods on the hill of Tara was badly damaged by British Zionists searching for the fabled Ark of the Covenant.

The Great Chicago Fire of 1871, the worst in
American history, left at least 300 people dead and
90,000 homeless, and caused $200,000,000 worth
of damage. It began in a barn in De Koven Street
when a cow owned by Mrs Patrick O'Leary kicked
a lighted lantern over some straw.

Ancient Irish kings were forbidden to go anywhere on their own. On private business, they had to be accompanied by nine retainers, on public business, at least twelve.

MOST of the horses involved in the ill-fated Charge of the Light Brigade came from the British Army's cavalry depot at Newbridge, County Kildare.

THE Flemish dialect Yola, which arrived in Ireland at the time of the Norman invasion, was spoken in the Forth district of County Wexford until the early 1800s.

THE Shackleton Ice Shelf in Antarctica is named after the Kildare-born explorer Sir Ernest Shackleton who came to within ninety-seven miles of the South Pole in 1908, the farthest south any man had been until that time.

THE first film shown in Ireland was screened by the Lumiere brothers at Dan Lowry's Music Hall (now the Olympia Theatre) in Dublin in 1896.

IN Galway in 1477, Christopher Columbus heard a story which so fired his imagination that it led to his discovery of the New World. He wrote in his journal that, 'Men of Cathay (China) have come east... in Galway... a man and a woman of extraordinary appearance have come to land on two tree trunks'. Scholars believe that they were probably Eskimos, whose kayaks had been blown there by a storm.

THE traditional game of road bowls was played not with iron balls but with the severed heads of English settlers following the destruction of the Munster plantation in 1598.

NOT all Irish boxers have been men. Mrs Stokes, the champion female pugilist of London's East End, challenged the city's Irish community to send 'Hibernian heroines' to meet her in single combat at Marylebone Fields.

THE Caribbean island of Montserrat is the world's 'other Emerald Isle'. Colonised in 1632 by Irish Catholics, the islanders celebrate St. Patrick's day, regard Guinness as their national drink, and have a shamrock on their passports.

CHRISTMAS cards were first mass-produced in the 1860s by the Belfast firm of Marcus Ward.

310,000-480,000 people out of a then population of some 2,400,000 died in the forgotten Irish famine of 1740-41, a proportionately greater number than perished during the Great Famine a century later.

IN an early instance of 'girl power', it was the custom, until the mid 19th century, for married women in County Westmeath to retain their maiden names.

Spirit-groceries were shops which sold groceries and served alcohol. Women who dared not enter the male-only world of the pub could use them to drown their sorrows while appearing to the outside world to be respectably engaged in shopping.

The Cave of Cats, near Rathcroghan, County Roscommon, was once believed to be the entrance to the Underworld.

THE quintessentially English game of croquet was first played in Ireland.

WILLIAM Hill-Walker, who founded the Irish National Stud at Tully, County Kildare in 1900, believed astrology could influence the outcome of races. He had skylights installed in his stables so that his horses could feel the full influence of the stars.

DUBLIN was a primarily protestant city until around the mid 18th century.

BUTTERMILK and potatoes, the staple diet in Ireland before the Famine, made the Irish peasantry the strongest and tallest in Europe, according to surgeons studying British Army recruits in the 1830s.

THE 'coffin ships' which carried Irish emigrants to the New World during the Famine were well named. At least sixty were sunk by collision, fire or storm. At least one in five who made the Atlantic crossing on them in 1847 succumbed to diseases picked up en route.

BETWEEN 1969-73 at least 60,000 people were displaced by the Troubles in Northern Ireland in what was, until that time, the biggest population movement in Europe since the Second World War.

EXTRACTS from a price list compiled during
the siege of Derry:

*A quarter of a dog (fattened by eating the bodies
of the slain Irish)*   5/6d
A dog's head   2/6d
A cat   4/6d
A rat   1 shilling

SO violent was the reaction to Synge's play *The
Playboy of the Western World* that five hundred
police had to be deployed around the Abbey
Theatre during its first run in 1907.

ABSOLUTE Zero (-273° Celsius), the lowest
temperature theoretically possible, was
discovered by Belfast-born scientist Lord Kelvin
in 1848.

DURING WW2 there were two different time
zones in Ireland. The neutral Free State held to
summer time, while Northern Ireland had
double summer time, giving an extra hour of
daylight for war production. This anomaly was
particularly confusing for rail passengers
travelling from Kesh in County Fermanagh to
Pettigo in County Donegal, who found
themselves completing their journey 45 minutes
before they had begun.

THE first Irish coins were minted by the
Vikings in 992.

The world has more than two thousand
Irish theme pubs.

In 1910 the Kalem Motion Picture Company
filmed melodramas in County Kerry for Irish-
American audiences. These films were the first to
feature the classic silent movie routine of the
villain tying the heroine to the railway track while
the hero races to save her.

THE first ever greyhound race was organised by an Irishman called Leary at Hendon on the then outskirts of London in 1876.

CONOR MacNessa, King of Ulster at the time of Christ, reputedly had a magical ball made of lime and human brains embedded in his forehead, which allowed him to see what was happening anywhere in the world.

£7,000,000 was spent on relief by the British government during the Great Famine.

THE first Irish cinema was The Volta, which opened in Dublin in 1909 under the management of one James Joyce.

WHEN Belfast and Dublin were linked by rail in 1855 the journey time between the two cities fell from three days to five hours.

Also available in the same series:

NEVER!
FASCINATING FACTS
about
IRELAND

Michael Smith
Illustrations: Nick Scott
ISBN 1 870132 65 3   £ 3.95